Pebble® Plus

CARS, CARS, CARS

BIG CARS

by Melissa Abramovitz

Gail Saunders-Smith, PhD, Consulting Editor

Consultant: Leslie Mark Kendall, Curator
Petersen Automotive Museum
Los Angeles, California

CAPSTONE PRESS
a capstone imprint

Pebble Plus is published by Capstone Press,
1710 Roe Crest Drive, North Mankato, Minnesota 56003.
www.capstonepub.com

Library of Congress Cataloging-in-Publication Data
Abramovitz, Melissa, 1954–
  Big cars / by Melissa Abramovitz.
      p. cm.—(Pebble plus. Cars, cars, cars)
  Summary: "Simple text and color photographs describe nine big cars"—Provided by the publisher.
  Includes bibliographical references and index.
  Audience: K-3.
  ISBN 978-1-62065-088-2 (library binding)
  ISBN 978-1-62065-869-7 (paperback)
  ISBN 978-1-4765-1072-9 (eBook PDF)
  1. Automobiles—Juvenile literature. 2. Limousines—Juvenile literature. I. Title. II. Series: Pebble plus. Cars, cars, cars.
  TL147.A277 2013
  629.222—dc23   2012031835

Editorial Credits
Erika L. Shores, editor; Kyle Grenz, designer; Laura Manthe, production specialist

Photo Credits
Alamy: Bob Masters Classic Car Images, 17; Dreamstime: Dikiiy, cover (right), 11; Getty Images: Heritage Images, 5, Michael Ochs Archives/Donaldson Collection, 21; Newscom: WENN Photos/ZDS/ZOB/GBAA, 7, ZUMA Press, 15; Shutterstock: 1xpert, design element, Walter G Arce, 19; Wikimedia: Craig Howell/CC Attribution 2.0 Generic, 13, IFCAR/public domain, cover (left), Josephew/CC BY-SA 3.0, 9

Note to Parents and Teachers

The Cars, Cars, Cars set supports national science standards related to science, technology, and society. This book describes and illustrates big cars. The images support early readers in understanding the text. The repetition of words and phrases helps early readers learn new words. This book also introduces early readers to subject-specific vocabulary words, which are defined in the Glossary section. Early readers may need assistance to read some words and to use the Table of Contents, Glossary, Read More, Internet Sites, and Index sections of the book.

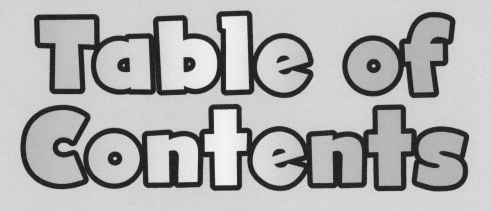

Table of Contents

Big

Stretch out your legs

or pack in the people.

Big cars have plenty of room!

Lincoln Town Cars are big,

comfortable cars.

Six people easily fit inside.

Size: 18.5 feet (5.6 meters) long;
4,129 pounds (1,873 kilograms)
Years sold: 1981 to 2011

The one-of-a-kind

Rolls-Royce Phantom 102EX

is the biggest electric car.

Power comes from a battery

and two electric motors.

Size: 19.16 feet (5.8 meters) long; 6,680 pounds (3,030 kilograms) One built in 2011

Before minivans, people drove
station wagons to carry a lot
of people. The longest station
wagons were Buick Estates.
Three roomy seats fit nine people.

Size: 19.26 feet (5.87 meters) long; 5,236 pounds (2,375 kilograms)
Years sold: 1974 to 1976

Bigger

Adding armor to Mercedes-Benz 770Ks made them the heaviest cars ever built. Armor and bulletproof windows kept passengers safe.

Size: 19.69 feet (6 meters) long;
10,582 pounds (4,800 kilograms)
Years sold: 1938 to 1943

Cadillac 452Ds were

the longest convertibles.

A powerful V-16 engine

made for a smooth ride.

Size: 20 feet (6.1 meters) long;
6,100 pounds (2,767 kilograms)
Years sold: 1934 to 1937

The longest passenger car sold today is the Maybach 62. This pricey car has leather seats, a TV, and a refrigerator.

Size: 20.2 feet (6.2 meters) long; 6,330 pounds (2,871 kilograms) Years sold: 2004 to present

Biggest

Giant Bugatti (boo-GAH-tee) Royales had an engine 5 feet (1.5 meters) long. Today only limousines top the size of a Royale.

Size: 21 feet (6.4 meters) long; 7,165 pounds (3,250 kilograms) Years sold: 1926 to 1933

Top fuel dragsters are
the longest, fastest race cars.
The ground shakes as dragsters
roar ahead at 330 miles
(531 kilometers) per hour.

Size: 25 feet (7.6 meters) long; 2,250 pounds (1,021 kilograms)

Jay Ohrberg built the biggest car ever. His limousine had 26 wheels. Helicopters could land on a helipad at the back.

Size: 100 feet (30.5 meters) long; unknown weight

Glossary

armor—a metal covering used to protect something

battery—a container holding chemicals that store and create electricity

bulletproof—something that has been made to protect people from bullets

convertible—a car with a top that can be put down

dragster—a car built to take part in drag races; in a drag race, two cars begin at a standstill and drive in a straight line at high speeds for a short distance

electric—powered by electricity

engine—a machine that makes the power needed to move something

helipad—a place where a helicopter can land or take off

limousine—a large, fancy car with a driver who is hired to take people to a certain place or special event

passenger—a person other than the driver in a car or vehicle

station wagon—a car with a large, closed-in cargo area behind the back seats, where the trunk would be

Read More

Adamson, Thomas K. *Dragsters.* Rev It Up! Mankato, Minn.: Capstone Press, 2011.

Doman, Mary Kate. *Cool Cars.* All about Big Machines. Berkeley Heights, N.J.: Enslow Elementary, 2012.

Gilpin, Daniel. *Record-Breaking Cars.* Record Breakers. New York: PowerKids Press, 2012.

Internet Sites

FactHound offers a safe, fun way to find Internet sites related to this book. All of the sites on FactHound have been researched by our staff.

Here's all you do:

Visit *www.facthound.com*

Type in this code: 9781620650882

Super-cool stuff! Check out projects, games and lots more at **www.capstonekids.com**

Index

Word Count: 191
Grade: 1
Early-Intervention Level: 23